WOODLAND HIGH SCHOOL
800 N. MOSELEY DRIVE
STOCKBRIDGE, GA. 30281
(770) 389-2784

World's **Worst** HISTORICAL DISASTERS

Chris McNab

WOODLAND HIGH SCHOOL
800 N. MOSELEY DRIVE
STOCKBRIDGE, GA. 30281
(770) 389-2784

ROSEN
PUBLISHING®

New York

This edition first published in 2009 by:

The Rosen Publishing Group, Inc.

29 E. 21st Street

New York, NY 10010

Project Editor: Sarah Uttridge

Picture Researcher: Terry Forshaw

Design: EQ Media

On the Cover: Foreground: Destruction caused by the Indian Ocean tsunami of December 2004. Background: Artist's rendering of the Great Fire of London of 1666.

Library of Congress Cataloging-in-Publication Data

McNab, Chris, 1970–

World's worst historical disasters / Chris McNab.

   p. cm.—(World's worst—from innovation to disaster)

Includes index.

ISBN-13: 978-1-4042-1843-7 (lib. binding)

1. Disasters—History. 2. Natural disasters—History. I. Title.

D24.M43 2009

363.3409—dc22

                       2008018022

Manufactured in the United States of America

Photo Credits

AKG Images: 18; Amber Books: 16, 17; Corbis: 35; Mary Evans Picture Library: 12, 21, 23, 24, 28, 31, 41, 45, 46, 52, 57; Getty Images: 15, 33, 61, 73, 74, 75; MARS/Art Tech: 39, 40, 47, 59; TRH Pictures: 62, 65, 66, 67, 69, 70, 71; U.S. Department of Defense: 51.

CONTENTS

INTRODUCTION

RECENT, APPALLING EVENTS IN THE INDIAN OCEAN HAVE REMINDED US HOW FRAGILE HUMAN BEINGS ARE UNDER THE POWERS OF NATURE, AND HOW ABRUPTLY AN ENTIRE WORLD REGION CAN GO FROM NORMALITY TO CATASTROPHE.

In the Western world, in particular, the comforting wrap of our relatively prosperous lives shields us from an uncomfortable historical truth – major disasters are common, recurrent features in almost every generation. Whether the disasters are caused by geological events, by social causes (war, riot etc.) or by industrial or mechanical accident, they cast a perpetual shadow.

NATURAL DISASTERS

In terms of sheer death toll, natural disasters have undoubtedly shown themselves as the most powerful calamities, rivaled only in death tolls by some of the world's largest wars. Natural disasters can be climatological, such as hurricanes, tornadoes, blizzards and flood; be geological, including earthquakes, volcanoes and landslides; or originate in famine and disease. When of sufficient magnitude, natural disasters often produce effects far beyond the immediate area they strike. The volcanic eruption that struck the Aegean island of Thera c.1650 not only removed huge amounts of the island's landmass but also caused a giant tsunami that devastated the coastline of Crete, an island located 70 miles (110 km) away. In this way the tsunami, not the volcanic eruption that caused it, is the most likely culprit in the downfall of one of the world's most impressive societies of the time.

HIGH DEATH TOLLS

As the Theran volcano illustrates, the effects of violent natural events can be terrifying. In 856, for example, an earthquake at the ancient city of Corinth killed an estimated 45,000 people in only a few seconds of tremors. Nor is such a death toll unusual. Even in the modern world earthquakes have catastrophic consequences – the earthquake in the Iranian city of Bam in 2003 killed 26,000 people, although many deaths occurred because housing was of traditional, fragile mud-brick and palm-trunk construction.

Yet if we were to talk crudely about the "worst" type of natural disaster, those involving flooding seem to generate disproportionately high death tolls. The final death toll of the Indian Ocean tsunami is likely to remain forever unknown, but it has reached over 225,000 fatalities. There are equally dreadful precedents. In 1970 an estimated half a million people died from storm flooding when a massive cyclone

➤➤

hit Bangladesh. An unfortunate pattern emerges from studying many natural disasters – those countries with high rates of poverty usually suffer from the greatest death tolls, as the housing structures and medical systems are ill equipped to cope with destructive physical events. In this light it is revealing that while 26,000 people died in Bam in 2003, "only" 3,000 died in the massive San Francisco earthquake back in 1906, most of the destruction from the latter event coming from subsequent fire rather than the tremors. In addition, while we identify a disaster with the exploding volcano or raging hurricane, for example, the twin destroyers, famine and disease, often compound that event in the aftermath.

FAMINE AND DISEASE

Of all the killers throughout human history, none approaches the sheer lethal effects of famine and disease. Often the two have followed in the wake of an initial disaster, such as a flood. Flooding carries particularly high risks of bringing long-term mortality in its wake, via several mechanisms. First of all sewerage and drinking-water systems are often mixed during floods, facilitating the spread of diseases such as cholera. Cholera results in rapid dehydration, and with the drinking water contaminated the affected people cannot implement the rehydration required to recover. The dead then further complicate the issue, corpses decomposing in the water systems also accelerate the spread of disease. The famine component of flooding disasters comes quite simply from ruined crops, but there is an added blow delivered by flooding from the sea. The salt deposits left by evaporated seawater are ruinous to fields for many years – in the early centuries the Romans used to sow enemy fields with salt as an act of war.

Of course, famine and disease do not need an inundation to take hold. Drought can precipitate awful famines, as the continent of Africa regularly experiences, and even human interference has caused horrific famine disasters. Between 1845 and 1851 Ireland suffered one of the worst famines known in all history, largely caused by land-use restrictions put in place by the British government. By the early 1850s, approximately 1.5 million people had perished because of the famine, and millions more were forced to leave Ireland, lest they starve to death, too. Many of those who left relocated to the United States. Famine struck China with equal ferocity between 1959 and 1961.

Like famines, diseases are often not treated as disasters unless they reach newsworthy magnitude. Diseases emerge slowly, over wide areas, and last for many years, even centuries. Such a development does not have the immediacy we associate with natural disasters, and yet diseases have proved to be among the most profound human calamities. Probably the greatest of all human disasters has been disease-related – during the Black Death of 1348–1351, the entire society of Europe was brought to

➤➤

the very edge of collapse by an epidemic that killed 75 million people, one-third of the continent's population.

MEDICAL UNDERSTANDING

Looking so far back in history, we might be consoled that such a horror could never be visited on the modern world, with its immeasurably greater medical understanding. Yet the confidence is unfortunately misplaced. Early in the twentieth century, the influenza pandemic of 1918–1919 killed an astonishing amount of people, around 70 million worldwide, despite there being good awareness of the methods of disease transmission. More recently, estimates of HIV/AIDS deaths in Africa alone have been projected at around 90 million by 2025. Even largely ignored tropical diseases such as malaria kill one million people every year. From such a perspective, natural disasters are not something that visits the human world every now and then, but phenomena that constantly roll on in different forms year after year and often result in unimaginable havoc and numerous horrendous deaths.

SOCIAL AND TECHNOLOGICAL DISASTERS

In many ways we are largely powerless to resist natural disasters, aside from preventative measures and effective disaster-response systems. Yet every year there are disasters caused by humankind itself, either through negligence or mechanical failure, or through willful destruction. There is a loose historical pattern to major disasters of this type. Prior to the industrial revolution of the eighteenth and nineteenth centuries, the primary vehicle for urban disasters caused by human beings was fire. The Great Fire of Rome in 64 CE broke out among the shopping stalls of the Circus Maximus and ended up gutting 10 of Rome's 14 districts. Sixteen hundred years later, London was devastated by a fire that destroyed 373 acres (150 hectares) of the city and more than 13,000 houses. The devastation wrought by the great fire of London and other fires in the seventeenth century inspired improvements in firefighting technology, including better manual pumps, fire hoses, and the first high-pressure fire engines. Nevertheless, fire continued to be the bane of people and property in cities both big and small. Two centuries after the London fire, for example, a raging inferno tore through Chicago, leaving that fast-growing city in tatters.

To this day, fire persists as a major cause of urban death, alongside other age-old social calamities such as riot and building collapse. Nonetheless the increasing presence of technological innovations, particularly in terms of travel, from the early 1800s has brought a whole new world of tragic potential alongside fresh liberties and benefits. Trains, airships, fixed-wing aircraft, high-rise buildings, spaceships, industrial manufacture – all have added to the variety of disaster that interrupts normal life. When such disasters occur, they do not have the gross death tolls that come with natural disasters, but on a localized scale they are just as hideous. The Bhopal gas disaster of 1984 has killed 20,000 people to date and has resulted in tens of thousands of birth defects and other health disorders. On occasions the number of fatalities is very small, but the poignant circumstances of the accident make the disaster worthy of such a title – the loss of the space shuttle Columbia in 2003 is one such example.

MANMADE DISASTERS

Human beings live in a world of risk, and as such accidental and natural disasters are part and parcel of the fabric of our existence, although that recognition makes them no less tragic when they occur. Far harder to rationalize are those disasters caused by intentional human agency. The 3,000 people who died in the September 11, 2001, attacks in the United States were part of a conscious desire to precipitate disaster – that the death toll probably exceeded the terrorists' intentions would have caused their leaders only increased satisfaction. During history's largest manmade disaster, World War II, an estimated 56 million people were killed, including 25 million Soviet citizens, 10 million Chinese and 6 million Jews. This global catastrophe can be traced back to the actions of just one or two people, something that attests to humankind's vulnerability before powerful individuals. Instances of deliberate disaster creation are included in this book, but they are relatively few and serve more to highlight the fact that conscious decision can be just as dangerous as negligence or nature.

The disasters charted here can make for grim reading, yet there is a glimmer of light. Humanity is still here and thriving, despite millennia of earthquakes, tornadoes, asteroid strikes, fires, tsunamis and pandemics. Viewed as such, disasters are as much a testimony to human durability as they are to human vulnerability.

ANCIENT DISASTERS 3000 BCE – 1 CE

Disasters loom large in the earliest recorded histories of humankind. By only the sixth book of Genesis in the Judeo-Christian scriptures, the writer gives account of a great flood that wipes out all people except those whom God permits to be saved. Other early religious writings contain similar disaster traditions. Apart from the perennial visitations from forces of war, the ancient world suffered predominantly from natural disasters, particularly earthquakes, volcanoes, tsunamis and disease. There is no doubt a catalogue of other contemporary disasters hidden from historical record, with the subsistence lifestyle of many ancient peoples leaving them very exposed to famine.

Left: The Cretan Tsunami created by a huge volcanic explosion on the Aegean island of Thera.

CRETAN TSUNAMI

A NATURAL DISASTER IN ONE LOCATION CAN PRECIPITATE A SUBSEQUENT, AND WORSE, DISASTER AT ANOTHER LOCATION. THE VOLCANO THAT ERUPTED *C*.1650 BCE ON THE ISLAND OF THERA IS A GOOD CASE IN POINT.

SHIFTING LANDMASS

Such was the sheer violence of the eruption that it literally blew the volcano and much of the island to pieces, removing about 32 square miles (82 square kilometers) of the island's landmass. The result was the formation of a caldera, essentially a bowl-shaped depression caused by the volcano collapsing in on itself. The surrounding Aegean Sea rushed to fill this huge depression, and the massive displacement of water combined with huge aquatic detonations as the seawater came into contact with the volcano's underlying magma. Radiating out from Thera came a tsunami measuring up to 492ft (150m) high and moving at around 100mph (160km/h).

Some 70 miles (110km) away from the Thera explosion was the northern coastline of Crete. Minoan Crete was at this time reaching the zenith of its cultural and political power, with great palace civilizations at locations such as Knossos and Mallia, both on the northern coast. When the wave struck Crete – the wall of water taking only minutes to cross the Aegean – massive damage was done to the Cretan ➤➤

Prior to the earthquake of 1650 BCE, Crete was one of the most powerful of the Greek islands. The tsunami generated from the Theran explosion rose to an estimated 492ft (150m) in height prior to its impact on the Cretan coastline.

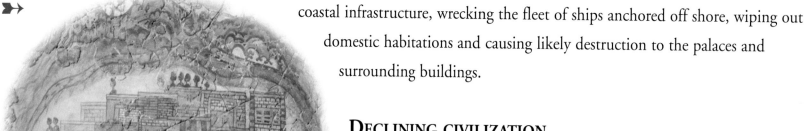

coastal infrastructure, wrecking the fleet of ships anchored off shore, wiping out domestic habitations and causing likely destruction to the palaces and surrounding buildings.

DECLINING CIVILIZATION

Archaeological finds also show that east Crete was choked by the vast clouds of pumice and ash drifting down from Thera, and this in turn led to great problems with agricultural pollution. Because the Theran eruption lies close to the beginnings of recorded history, there is no way of assessing casualty figures. However, what is known is that the decline of Minoan Crete's palace period is dated from around the time of the eruption, so it is likely that the volcano not only destroyed much of Thera but also brought about the disruption and decline of one of the most advanced civilizations of the time. ■

Above: A depiction of the advanced coastal cultures typical of Greece during the second millennium BCE. Coastlines have traditionally attracted the bulk of human urban development, which is one reason why tsunamis cause such a huge loss of life.

Ash clouds from a volcano have an enormous environmental impact. Not only do the deposits choke plant growth and affect the availability of animal food but the airborne clouds blot out the sun and cause a drop in temperatures as well.

IMPERIAL DISASTERS 1 CE – 1000

The growth of city cultures provided one of the key ingredients for a major disaster – large concentrations of people confined in relatively small areas of land. The catastrophic volcanic eruption of Vesuvius in 79 CE would have been a relatively minor affair had it occurred in a sparsely populated agricultural area. Instead, the volcano's pyroclastic flows struck Herculaneum, Pompeii and Stabiae, killing thousands of people instantly. Cities also brought the danger of fire, as open flames served for light, heat and cooking, and buildings were usually constructed of highly flammable natural materials.

Left: The spectacular eruption of Mount Vesuvius in 79 CE destroyed settlements and caused despair throughout the surrounding region.

POMPEII

IN 79 CE, THE CITIZENS OF POMPEII HAD LIVED IN THE SHADOW OF MOUNT VESUVIUS FOR HUNDREDS OF YEARS.

The volcano was actually a blessing – the fertile volcanic soil gave the area excellent agricultural growth. However, on August 24 the volcano finally turned on Pompeii's citizens.

WARNING SIGNS

The eruption had been preceded by several days of geological phenomena. There were minor earth tremors, as well as significant changes in the flow speed and levels of nearby watercourses. Animals were also behaving strangely, with dogs, cats and livestock seeming agitated. Finally, in the early afternoon of the 24th, Vesuvius erupted with a massive explosion. The first stage of the eruption saw a gargantuan cloud of pumice, rocks and ash climb as high as 12 miles (20km) into the atmosphere, then begin to settle back onto the ground. These deposits fell in a thick, scalding-hot blanket on Pompeii's streets, 6 miles (10km) away from Vesuvius, at a rate of 6in (15cm) per hour. The citizens of another town, Herculaneum, were actually nearer the eruption, but escaped the ash by being downwind. Although a number of people were killed by falling rocks and asphyxiation in Pompeii, the greatest danger was the build-up of ash crushing homes with its weight. For eight hours, the ash kept falling, stacking up to a height of 8–10ft (2–4m). Thousands of the city's people evacuated and

KEY FACTS

August 24, 79, 1:30 P.M. – Mount Vesuvius erupts, creating a vast cloud of tephra (volcanic emissions), which falls on Pompeii for around eight hours.

Huge ash deposits on Pompeii crush many buildings.

11:30 P.M. – A succession of pyroclastic flows begins from the volcano and wipes out Herculaneum, Stabiae and Pompeii.

Pompeii's ruins are now a major tourist attraction. The massive output of volcanic emissions submerged much of the city in ash deposits, and these served to preserve the ruins for future generations.

headed out into the countryside, leaving only an unfortunate 10 percent of the population behind.

SCORCHED EARTH

Night came, the darkness showing up a spectacular fireworks display from Vesuvius. Shortly before midnight, the nature of the eruption tragically changed. The huge column of superheated debris rising from the volcano began to collapse, and turned into a pyroclastic flow of molten pumice and rock, which rolled down the volcano side at hundreds of miles an hour and temperatures of 750°F (398°C). Herculaneum was engulfed and razed, along with all inhabitants, in a matter of seconds. Further flows fell short of Pompeii, until a final blast at 6:30 A.M. wiped the city from the face of the earth, the 2,000 citizens being scalded and asphyxiated to death in seconds. Both Herculaneum, Pompeii and nearby Stabiae were buried under tons of concrete-hard ash, in places up to 65ft (20m) deep. Vesuvius has erupted nearly 500 times since 79 CE, and today threatens the huge Italian city of Naples, with its population of more than one million. ■

The open countryside was one of the few places of safety during the eruption of Mount Vesuvius in 79 CE, although a distance of just several miles from the volcano was enough to ensure protection from the pyroclastic flows.

MEDIEVAL DISASTERS 1000 – 1500

The medieval world was struck by disaster on a global scale in the form of the Black Death. This horrific killer, which took the lives of one in three Europeans, showed how terribly vulnerable the human race was to a disease that was easily transmitted and against which there was no immunity. Lethal disease is a constant visitor to the medieval period, and the beginnings of transoceanic colonization in the fifteenth century ensured that European diseases were exported globally, often with devastating effects upon the indigenous populations. A drop in global temperatures, beginning what is known as the Little Ice Age, also added to a time of great social trauma.

Left: Scenes from the horrific Black Death, which killed
up to 33 percent of the entire population of Europe.

BLACK DEATH

THE ORIGINS OF THE BLACK DEATH ARE DIFFICULT TO ASCERTAIN, BUT IT APPEARS TO HAVE STARTED IN CHINA IN THE EARLY 1330S AND SPREAD VIA TRADE ROUTES THROUGH TO ASIA, THEN WESTERN EUROPE, WHERE IT STRUCK IN 1348.

The disease came in three basic varieties, all with acute mortality rates. Bubonic plague, named after the swellings (buboes) that appeared on the victim's body, had a 30–75 percent mortality rate and was spread by rat fleas; pneumonic plague, with a rate of 90–95 percent, was an airborne disease transmitted in the same way as influenza; and septicemic plague caused acute blood poisoning and had a mortality rate of 99–100 percent.

APOCALYPSE

Whatever the type of disease, the plague turned medieval Europe into a charnel house. It is hard to overstate the social impact of the Black Death. Entire households and communities could go from healthy to dead in a matter of a few days, sometimes overnight. Whole cities lost around 50 percent of their inhabitants, urban areas being the most vulnerable to the disease because of overcrowding and poor sanitation. Households infected with the plague were quarantined – and, in Milan, the authorities walled up diseased families in their own homes, a measure ➤➤

KEY FACTS

1330s – Plague originates in China and spreads to western Europe by 1348.

1348–51 – One-third of the European population dies from the effects of the plague, a total of around 75 million people, which had a catastrophic effect on the social, religious and economic fabric of society.

Religious rites were a rarity for the dead and the dying during the plague years. Most of the victims were buried in huge plague pits outside the city walls, many of which are still visible today in Europe.

Black Rat.

Above: The rat flea was the principal source of the Black Death, but over the centuries the disease mutated into several other lethal forms, including an airborne pneumonic form that had a 90 percent mortality rate.

that resulted in Milan having one of the best records of controlling the disease within a large urban population.

NIGHTMARE WORLD

Bodies littered the streets in vast quantities. The writer of the *Decameron*, Giovanni Boccaccio, recorded that "Dead bodies filled every corner . . . Although the cemeteries were full, they [the local people] were forced to dig huge trenches, where they buried the bodies by hundreds." The art of the period commonly shows the figure of death riding through an apocalyptic landscape on a skeletal horse, and social order teetered on total collapse.

The Black Death is arguably the greatest natural disaster in all of human history. Between 1348 and 1351, the plague killed up to 33 percent of the entire population of Europe, a total of around 75 million people, and it would strike down millions more in future outbreaks throughout medieval and early modern history. ∎

SPANISH COLONIZATION

THE SPANISH COLONIZATION OF THE AMERICAS RESULTED IN ONE OF THE GREATEST PERIODS OF SOCIAL, HUMAN AND CULTURAL DESTRUCTION IN HISTORY.

The drive for a Spanish empire began roughly around 1469, when Ferdinand V of Castile and Isabella I of Aragon married to bring Spain under the rule of a single monarchical house. With internal politics consolidated, the Spanish now began to look outward to the formation of an empire.

ENTERING THE AMERICAS

From 1492, when Christopher Columbus made landings on the Caribbean islands, until around 1518, the Spanish consolidated the Caribbean and began pushing outward into central and southern America. A key element in their colonial expansion was the *conquistadores,* explorer soldiers who became as noted for their cruelty as for their undoubted bravery. Two *conquistadores* in particular stand out for the effect they had on the indigenous American people. One of them was the infamous Hernán Cortés. In 1518, he took a small army up into Mexico, and by 1521 he had brought about the destruction of the entire Aztec empire, massacring tens of thousands of its people at places such as Cholula and the Aztec capital, Tenochtitlán. In the same way that the Aztec civilization was destroyed, the ➤➤

KEY FACTS

- **1490s** – Spain begins the process of colonizing the New World.
- **The colonization** results in the destruction of some of the Americas' major civilizations, including the Aztecs of Mexico and the Incas of Peru.
- **Around 45 million** native Americans die from diseases introduced by the Spanish.

conquistadores of an equally famous explorer, Francisco Pizarro, crushed the Inca empire of Peru during the 1530s, and in 1572 the last of the Inca rulers was beheaded.

COLONIAL DESTRUCTION

Mexico and Peru are but two examples of the excesses of Spanish colonization in the Americas, and military massacres were unfortunately common during the expansion. However, it was not the *conquistadores* themselves who had the most devastating impact on the continent, but the non-indigenous diseases that they introduced, particularly smallpox, measles and influenza. For example, the Aztecs were not only militarily overwhelmed, but were also felled by a smallpox epidemic: around three million died, one-third of the Aztec population. More than 100,000 Incas were killed by the disease in Cuzco, their capital, alone. Estimates for the total disease-related death toll in the Americas between 1500 and 1650 has been placed at around 45 million, which represents around 90 percent of the indigenous population. The world has rarely seen such enormous cultural destruction since. ∎

Above: New developments in transoceanic maritime technology and navigation in the sixteenth century made colonization possible.

The native Indians had once presided over huge internal empires, but most were forced into slavery after the Spanish conquests, with cruel working conditions compounding the effects of introduced diseases.

SLAVERY IN THE AMERICAS

THE TRANSATLANTIC SLAVE TRADE WAS A PHENOMENON AS DURABLE AS IT WAS TERRIBLE, BEGINNING AROUND THE MID-FIFTEENTH CENTURY AND LASTING UNTIL THE 1800s.

It began in 1444, when the Portuguese opened trading relations with the west coast of Africa and began extracting around 800 slaves a year to fill gaps in its domestic agricultural labor market.

HUMAN RESOURCES

By the mid-sixteenth century, however, Spain, Britain and the Netherlands had joined the trade, using African slave labor in the burgeoning European colonies in the Americas. This new market led to a huge expansion in the numbers of slaves required, and about 15,000 a year made the long and harrowing voyage across the Atlantic by the 1600s. Most ended up in the Caribbean or mainland Latin/South America, where they were placed in abusive servitude on plantations (two-thirds of all African slaves would work in sugar plantations) or in mining.

North America received its first batch of slaves in 1619 in Virginia, and what was to be the southern United States ultimately became one of the biggest beneficiaries of the slave trade. Although the imported peoples initially had some on-paper rights under conditions of "limited servitude," these were legally and practically eroded until conditions of full slavery were enshrined in most southern regions.

KEY FACTS

An estimated 10 million African slaves were exported to the Americas from the late 1400s to the early 1800s.

A low estimate of fatalities aboard the slave ships is two million dead, although some suggest a figure of up to 10 million.

Slavery in the United States is finally terminated following the US Civil War (1861–65).

A horrifying though sanitized impression of a slave ship. Such ships would have had limited ventilation, while toilet facilities consisted of little more than a bucket in the corner of the hold.

During the 1700s, Great Britain was the biggest supplier of slaves to the New World, shipping around 50,000 slaves a year. It abolished slave trading in 1807, but the United States retained 893,000 slaves and smuggled in up to 15,000 a year despite Congressional prohibitions on importation from 1808. Only the civil war of 1861–65 overthrew the institution, and even then African-Americans would remain persecuted and segregated in many sectors of American society up until the 1960s.

SHIPS OF DEATH

The crimes committed during the 400 years of the transatlantic slave trade were truly awful. Around 10 million Africans were transported abroad. On the basis of surviving ships' records, it is estimated that some two million died during transit to the Americas; mortality on the slave ships during the mid-1700s ran at around 20–29 percent. Yet this estimate could be conservative. Those who reached their destination faced a life of unrelenting labor and frequent cruelty, with a short life expectancy. ∎

Above: The king of the Congo welcomes the Portuguese colonizers in the mid-fifteenth century. Congo soon became a major center of slave exportation, the Europeans making local rulers wealthy through their complicity in gathering and processing slaves.

The route to slavery actually began among the African peoples themselves, and many North African rulers actively traded human beings with the colonists and European/American adventurers.

EARLY MODERN DISASTERS 1500 – 1700

The Early Modern period saw a huge expansion in the sum of human knowledge, and a new level of sophistication of science, art, architecture and theology. However, the elemental forces of nature remained just as strong. Great cities were almost wiped out in cataclysmic events, with Lisbon destroyed by earthquake and tsunami in 1531 with the loss of 70,000 lives, and London gutted by fire in 1666. Furthermore, despite the growth of conspicuous wealth within the cities, the majority of the world's population remained as agricultural poor, and they were as vulnerable to natural disaster as ever.

Left: The fire of London in 1666 burnt for three days and destroyed 13,000 houses.

FIRE OF LONDON

IN THE SUMMER OF 1666, LONDON WAS A CITY SIMPLY INVITING A DEVASTATING FIRE. ITS PHYSICAL STRUCTURE WAS A FIREFIGHTER'S NIGHTMARE – CLOSE-PACKED WOOD-FRAMED HOUSES ARRANGED ALONG NARROW STREETS, WITH MANY OF THESE POSSESSING OVERHANGING UPPER FLOORS.

The danger was increased by the strong, dry southeasterly wind that frequented the city, and the summer had been a particularly hot one, making woodwork even more flammable and reducing water levels in rivers and ponds.

THE FIRE STARTS

Many individuals had already recognized the danger of London being devastated by fire. Even the king, Charles II, had expressed concerns at such a possibility.

However, all warnings went unheeded and, in the early hours of September 2, 1666, Thomas Farynor, the king's baker, awoke in his house on Pudding Lane (close to London Bridge) to the smell of burning. A fire had started downstairs, and it quickly spread through the house, forcing the family to escape via the roof – a maid stayed downstairs and would die in the fire.

The fire spread to nearby buildings with alarming rapidity. It was unable to cross the London Bridge, but instead concentrated itself in the City of London. By the end of the morning, huge swathes of central London were in flames. Charles II ordered London mayor Sir Thomas Bloodworth to begin tearing down buildings to create firebreaks, but such measures were ineffective, with the fire leaping more than 100ft (32m) in places.

➤

KEY FACTS

London's layout and wood-framed buildings made the city an acute fire hazard.

Fire starts at 2:00 A.M. on September 2, 1666, in Pudding Lane, and spreads through the City of London by the next morning.

Fire burns for three days, destroying 373 acres (150 hectares) of London.

Panicked citizens of London take to the river Thames in an attempt to escape the fire sweeping through the city. Tradition has given the fire of London a low death toll, but recent historical studies suggest the possibility of thousands of fatalities.

➤➤

INFERNO

One day later, and the fire had spread through some of London's most populous districts, such as Gracechurch Street, Cheapside and around the Royal Exchange. St Paul's Cathedral was not spared, and even its lead roof was melted. The rising smoke could be seen by people living in Oxford, about 55 miles (90km) away. The fire kept spreading until September 5, when a change in wind strength and direction, and an effective use of firebreaks, saw the fire contained, then allowed to burn itself out. The devastation wrought on the structure of London was profound – 373 acres (150 hectares) of city burnt and more than 13,000 houses destroyed. The registered death toll was only four people, but many recent historians consider that the actual toll would have been far higher, as the heat of the flames would have reduced corpses to ash. Indeed, eyewitnesses reported a prevalent odor of burnt flesh. Although many Londoners accused foreigners of starting the fire, there is no real evidence to suggest a cause other than an accident. ■

Above: Seventeenth-century London's close-packed housing enabled the fire to spread rapidly. Organized firefighting was almost absent, and at the height of the blaze gunpowder charges were used to literally blast down houses and create instant firebreaks.

The fire may have devastated the City of London, but an unexpected bonus of the conflagration was that it killed off much of the city's rat population, thereby helping to reduce the incidences of plague.

INDUSTRIAL AGE DISASTERS 1700 – 1900

The major disasters of the eighteenth and nineteenth centuries are generally little different from those of preceding centuries, there being the regular episodes of earthquakes, volcanic eruptions and other natural events. However, enormous population growth during these centuries meant that the death tolls from famine and disease easily climbed into the millions. The technological revolution also brought with it new engines of transportation and warfare, and intensified methods of industrial production and mining. These in turn created a whole new potential for catastrophic events.

Left: The great Chicago fire of 1871 gave much
of the city the appearance of a terrible war zone.

IRISH POTATO FAMINE

THE IRISH POTATO FAMINE OF 1845–51 REMAINS A SHAMEFUL EPISODE IN BRITISH HISTORY, DESPITE THE FACT THAT THE FAMINE ORIGINATED FROM NATURAL CAUSES.

In the 1800s, the potato was the staple food of around 50 percent of the Irish population, essential to their subsistence lifestyle. Part of the problem lay in the fact that the British government restricted most farmers to around 5 acres (2 hectares) of land, and potatoes gave a greater yield on these small plots than grain.

CROP FAILURE

During the harvest of 1845, the potato crop was hit by a destructive fungus, *Phytophtora infestans,* the effect of which was to accelerate the decay of the potato once it was infected. After only a few days, the potato became blackened, rotting, slimy and completely inedible. Horrifically, the fungus swept through 50 percent of the potato crop of 1845, but wiped out almost the entire crop of 1846. The poor of Ireland were plunged into starvation.

The famine in Ireland was of biblical proportions, with more than one million people dead by the early 1850s, starved or killed by associated disease. Contemporary commentators report seeing skeletal orphaned children hopelessly begging for food, and huge pits for corpses ready for mass burial.

KEY FACTS

1845–51 – Ireland experiences a catastrophic failure of the potato crop, a food on which 50 percent of the population rely for existence.

The British government responses are generally uncaring and inadequate, and more than one million people die of starvation and disease.

Some three million people emigrate from Ireland to the United States during the famine.

➤➤

A priest comforts a family during the Irish potato famine. For those who did not die during the famine, emigration to the United States was a desirable option, where people were not faced with the land ownership strictures imposed by the British in Ireland.

Above: The people of 19th century Ireland were acutely dependent upon the potato as a food crop, with meat and other vegetables rare for the rural poor.

POOR RESPONSE

The response of the British government was inadequate. At first, Sir Robert Peel's conservative government imported Indian meal, but many of the starving were too poor to be able to afford the food. In 1848, the Whig government provided soup kitchens, but these were inadequate and were then stopped because the government perceived improvements in that year's crop yield. The yield per acre did improve in 1847, but there was less land being cultivated so the famine remained, and was increased again by almost complete crop failure in 1848. To earn a living, many people were channeled into workhouses, but conditions for the weakened people were so appalling that almost 200,000 people died in these institutions.

The Irish potato famine had two important social effects. First of all, it encouraged mass emigration, with around three million Irish people fleeing to the United States between 1845 and 1870. Among those left behind, the memory of the famine fostered an intense Irish nationalism, in turn feeding political violence which lasts to this day. ■

The potato famine brought death on an unimaginable scale to the Irish people. At its height, the famine resulted in parish churches letting the dead go unburied so that they could buy food and clothing for the poor instead of coffins.

THE GREAT CHICAGO FIRE

BY 1871, CHICAGO WAS DEVELOPING AT A FRENETIC PACE. AS ONE OF THE FASTEST-GROWING CITIES IN THE UNITED STATES, CHICAGO WAS PACKED WITH CHEAP WOODEN HOUSING THAT WAS CONSTRUCTED USING QUESTIONABLE BUILDING STANDARDS, PRESENTING A SEVERE FIRE HAZARD.

The risk of fire was exacerbated by a three-week lack of rain. Indeed, rainfall over the summer of 1871 had been a quarter of normal levels, so the danger of fire was great.

THE FIRE IGNITES

On October 8, 1871, a fire started around the barn of a Mrs. O'Leary on De Koven Street on the west side of the Chicago River. Fanned by warm, strong southwesterly winds, the fire quickly took hold, leaping across houses and factories at a terrifying rate. Soon a large section of the west side was on fire, and the flames leapt the river to set the east side ablaze, too (pollution of the Chicago River caused the surface of the water itself to ignite in many places). Soon many great and famous buildings were reduced to ashes, including the Tribune Building, the Palmer and Sherman hotels, and the city courthouse, which collapsed with a roar ➤➤ that was heard more than 1 mile (1.6km) away. The State Street Bridge burned up

KEY FACTS

October 8, 1871 – Fire starts in De Koven Street, Chicago, and quickly spreads out across the city, crossing the Chicago River at several points.

October 10 – The fire finally burns itself out, having destroyed an area of nearly 4 square miles (10.4 square kilometers) and killed around 300 people.

The Chicago fire of 1871 gave much of the city the appearance of a war zone. The heavy use of wood in the city's construction, including the use of wood paving in many places, dramatically increased Chicago's incendiary properties.

➤➤

Above: The flames and smoke of the Chicago fire could be seen from miles away. The riverside areas suffered extremely badly owing to the presence of lumberyards, warehouses full of flammable materials, and the presence of fuel for the ships.

and allowed the fire to spread to the north side. By this time the city's population was in total panic, a situation worsened by the presence of gangs of looters taking advantage of the social chaos.

QUENCHING THE FIRE

The Chicago fire burned for two whole days before, finally, heavy downpours of rain helped the fire to burn itself out. The fire had destroyed nearly 4 square miles (10.4 sq km). An estimated 300 people had been killed (the official death toll was 125, but many bodies were not found) and 18,000 buildings were lost, leaving one-third of the population homeless, a total of 100,000 people. Legend has gathered around the cause of the fire, the popular version being that Mrs. O'Leary's cow kicked over a lantern in her barn, although some evidence points to one Daniel Sullivan setting fire to the barn while stealing milk. However, while there is little dispute as to the source of the fire, the actual cause may never be known with certainty. ■

Survivors of the Chicago fire inspect the tremendous damage done to the city's infrastructure.

DISASTERS OF A NEW CENTURY 1900 – 1945

The first half of the twentieth century was dominated by two global disasters in the form of two world wars. These wars killed more than 70 million people, with World War II accounting for far more civilian deaths than military fatalities. Human activity causes an alarming high proportion of the world's calamities in this period. Yet the wars did not leave the world exempt from other forms of disaster. For example, earthquakes and flooding continued to cause widespread death and destruction. In addition, society was still reeling from the effects of World War I when the influenza pandemic of 1918–1919 struck, killing more than 70 million people.

Left: Together, the earthquake and resulting fire that devastated San Francisco in 1906 are remembered as one of the worst disasters in US history.

SAN FRANCISCO EARTHQUAKE

THE SAN FRANCISCO EARTHQUAKE OF 1906 STANDS AS THE UNITED STATES' GREATEST GEOLOGICAL DISASTER.

In 1906, the population of the city was around 400,000, a population precariously balanced upon the San Andreas fault.

POWERFUL TREMORS

On April 18, 1906, at 5:12 A.M., the city was awakened by a powerful earth tremor, which quickly subsided. Twenty seconds later, all hell broke loose as the San Andreas fault ruptured along 267 miles (430km) of its length, with the epicenter concentrated on the city itself. The earthquake lasted for about 45 seconds, with the ground being displaced 20ft (6m) in places, and the magnitude of the quake registered around 7.7 on the Richter scale. In the 45 seconds it shook, the city of San Francisco was wrecked: buildings collapsed; water mains split apart; people died both in their homes and out in the streets, where they were killed by lethal blocks of falling rubble. Yet although huge devastation occurred in less than one minute of tremors, the disaster was to be prolonged over three days by the huge fires that broke out across the city, fueled by fractured gas lines. The fire burned for a total of three days, during which time it incinerated an area of around 4.7 square miles (12.1 square kilometers) before it was finally brought under control.

After the fire came the grim task of damage assessment. The total number of buildings destroyed was 28,188. Revealingly, only 3,168 of that figure was accounted for by brick-built houses, the remainder of the total indicating how appallingly ➤➤

KEY FACTS

April 18, 1906, 5:12 A.M. – San Francisco experiences an initial tremor, followed 20 seconds later by a massive 45-second earthquake measuring 7.7 on the Richter scale.

The earthquake and a resulting three-day fire kill around 3,000 people, leave 225,000 homeless and cost $400 million.

San Francisco's precipitous streets aided the passage of the fire that resulted from the earthquake, as the flames traveled more easily along uphill routes. This photograph was taken by Arnold Genthe from the top of Sacramento Street and clearly shows the fire advancing towards the onlookers.

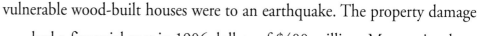

vulnerable wood-built houses were to an earthquake. The property damage had a financial cost in 1906 dollars of $400 million. More seriously, more than half of the city's entire population – 225,000 people – were rendered homeless. They, however, could be classed as the lucky ones. Although precise figures for the final death toll are difficult to ascertain, it is likely that around 3,000 people died during the earthquake and subsequent fire.

FUTURE TREMORS?

Today, the city of San Francisco remains astride the San Andreas fault, which according to most scientists has a typical main eruption cycle of once every 200 years. However, significant tremors may occur well before 2106 and, with San Francisco's population at 750,000, the consequences of another major earthquake could be even more profound than the 1906 event. ■

Above: San Francisco's physical structure was severely destabilized by the earth tremors, particularly among those buildings located close to the fault rupture. However, the greatest portion of the destruction visited upon the city came from the resultant fire.

The earthquake was caused by a rupture along the northern end of the San Andreas fault, extending for 267 miles (430km).

INFLUENZA PANDEMIC

BETWEEN 1918 AND 1919, THE WORLD WAS GRIPPED BY A DISEASE THAT KILLED AN ESTIMATED 70 MILLION PEOPLE, MAKING THE PANDEMIC SECOND ONLY TO THE BUBONIC PLAGUE OF THE MIDDLE AGES IN TERMS OF VIRULENCE AND DEATH TOLL.

The influenza pandemic had its origins in the trenches of the Western Front during the last year of World War I (1914–1918). A severe flulike illness started to afflict Allied soldiers in France in the spring of 1918, although they usually recovered in less than two weeks. However, by midsummer the symptoms of the illness had intensified, causing pneumonia, septicemia and organ failure, with about a 30 percent fatality rate. In the US Army, a total of 43,000 servicemen died of the illness in Europe.

GLOBAL KILLER

The disease – often known historically as "Spanish flu" despite the fact that the disease was probably imported from the United States, not Spain – was startlingly contagious, and soon spread from military to civilian communities around the world. More than 400,000 German civilians died during 1918 alone, and it reached the United Kingdom in May, killing 230,000 people by the beginning ➤➤

KEY FACTS

Disease begins on the battlefields of France in the spring of 1918.

More than 70 million people die of the influenza over the next two years.

Disease appears to be most lethal against those aged from 20 to 40 years.

Highest death toll in India – 16 million fatalities.

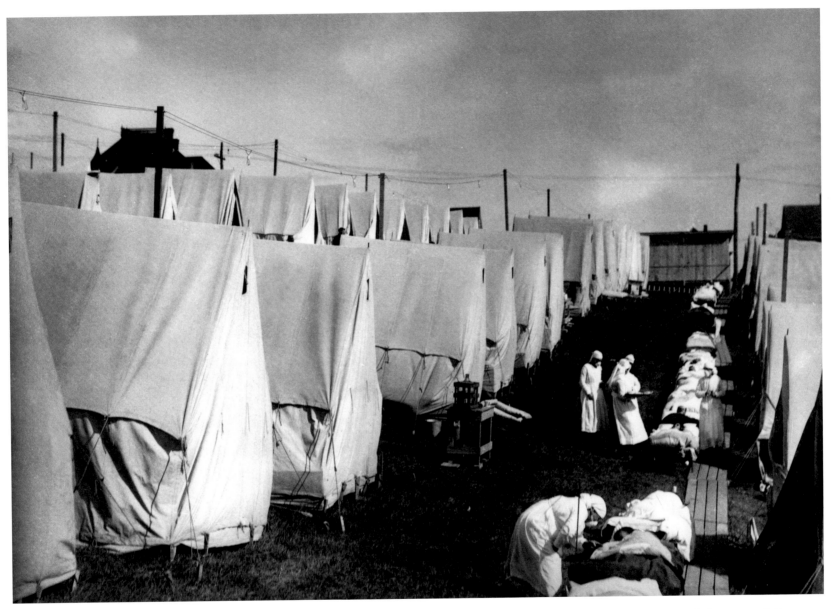

During the influenza pandemic, emergency treatment and isolation centers were set up throughout Europe and the United States. A basic understanding of disease transmission prevented the disease becoming a second Black Death in the West.

➠

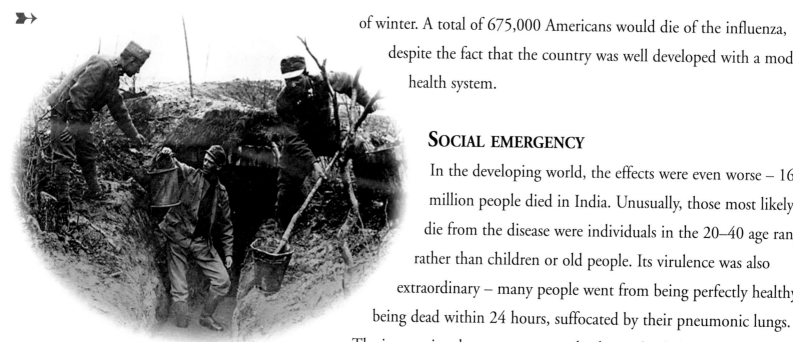

Above: The influenza pandemic originated in the unsanitary conditions of the Western Front at the end of World War I. A general state of poor health among many of the war-weary soldiers would have suppressed immune systems and facilitated the spread of the disease.

of winter. A total of 675,000 Americans would die of the influenza, despite the fact that the country was well developed with a modern health system.

SOCIAL EMERGENCY

In the developing world, the effects were even worse – 16 million people died in India. Unusually, those most likely to die from the disease were individuals in the 20–40 age range, rather than children or old people. Its virulence was also extraordinary – many people went from being perfectly healthy to being dead within 24 hours, suffocated by their pneumonic lungs.

The international emergency completely overloaded medical resources and mortuaries. In the United States, special flu ordinances included restrictions on travel, the distribution of gauze face masks, the banning of sales in department stores and even time limits placed on the length of funeral gatherings (only 15 minutes). The pandemic subsided towards the end of 1919, but today scientists are aware of the potential for new strains of influenza to have equally devastating effects. ∎

A court conducts its proceedings outdoors as part of a wave of measures to prevent the spread of the influenza virus. The death toll from the pandemic was greatest in the developing world, where poverty and close-packed housing ensured a rapid infection rate.

MODERN DISASTERS
1945 – PRESENT DAY

The world has seen more technological revolution since 1945 than it witnessed in all the preceding centuries put together. While much of this technology, particularly in areas of computerization and transport, has immeasurably improved life, it has also provided the ingredients for hi-tech disaster. Space exploration remains a dangerous pursuit, illustrated by the loss of two space shuttles and numerous other space vehicles in airborne or launch-pad accidents. The Bhopal gas disaster (1984) is a further example of how human beings often cannot control what they create.

Left: The September 11 attacks on the United States are one of the most important world events of the twenty-first century.

BHOPAL

THE BHOPAL DISASTER OF DECEMBER 1984 WAS A MAJOR INDUSTRIAL CATASTROPHE. ACCORDING TO SUBSTANTIATED REPORTS, IT HAS KILLED A TOTAL OF 20,000 PEOPLE TO DATE AND LEFT ANOTHER 120,000 WITH SERIOUS HEALTH PROBLEMS.

The journey to the disaster has its beginnings in the 1970s, when the US-based Union Carbide company established a pesticide factory in the city of Bhopal, India. Owing to the poverty of most of India's farmers, the Bhopal factory ceased to be profitable, and production ceased in the 1980s. However, as the factory contained a mix of highly lethal chemicals, it retained a staff who oversaw storage and safety. All evidence now suggests that the factory was allowed to lapse into disrepair, with corrosion eating into valves, pipes and storage tanks.

DISASTER WAITING TO HAPPEN

On the night of December 2/3, 1984, as an employee was flushing out a rusted pipe, several safety valves ruptured and allowed water to flow into a tank of the chemical methyl isocyanate (MIC). The ingress of water resulted in an explosion in the tank, and an enormous cloud of lethal MIC gas, and a number of other dangerous chemicals, was released into the air to settle over the densely packed housing of Bhopal.

➤➤

KEY FACTS

December 2/3, 1984 – A fractured storage tank at the Union Carbide pesticide plant in Bhopal, India, releases a huge cloud of lethal chemicals over the city.

Up to 15,000 people die in the first week of the disaster, most from asphyxiation and/or damage to the nervous system.

The people of Bhopal continue to suffer from unusually high rates of cancer, respiratory illness, gynecological disorders, birth defects and blindness.

The gases released from the Union Carbide plant were highly aggressive to eye tissue. Thousands of people were completely or partially blinded, and only a lucky few regained their former vision.

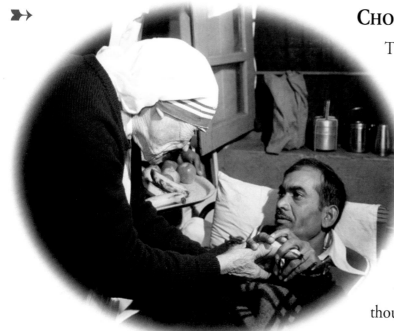

Above: Mother Teresa comforts a Bhopal victim. A survivor described the overwhelming effects of the gas: "It felt like somebody had filled our bodies up with red chillies, our eyes had tears coming out, noses were watering, we had froth in our mouths."

CHOKING GAS

The effect was horrific. Thousands of people woke with severe choking and asphyxiation. Distraught crowds filled the streets, where bodies were already beginning to pile up. People went blind and died as their lungs filled with fluid, or from convulsions as the chemicals attacked their nervous systems. Estimates for the first week's death toll run from 8,000 to 15,000. Yet although the gas dispersed a few days after the initial explosion, people have continued to die in Bhopal from related cancers, respiratory illnesses and brain disorders, and thousands of women have given birth to hideously deformed children. Bhopal is saturated in dangerous substances – levels of mercury in underground water, for example, were found to be up to six million times normal levels. Although the Union Carbide company has paid out $470 million in compensation (very little considering that 500,000 people were exposed), its senior management has effectively escaped criminal prosecution. ∎

Funeral pyres ran constantly in the aftermath of the Bhopal disaster. Corpse disposal became a major problem, as incidences of disease increased. To date, an estimated 20,000 people have died from the initial or long-term effects of the gas.

SEPTEMBER 11 ATTACKS

THE SEPTEMBER 11 ATTACKS STAND AS ONE OF THE MOST IMPORTANT WORLD EVENTS OF THE TWENTY-FIRST CENTURY.

The tragedy began on the morning of September 11, 2001. A total of nineteen terrorists, all connected to the Islamic group al-Qaeda, boarded four commercial airliners, two flying out of Boston, one from Washington DC and the fourth from Newark, New Jersey. Once the aircraft were airborne, the hijackers took them over and seated themselves at the controls. (Some of the terrorists had undergone flight training in United States.)

DEVASTATING ATTACK

At 8:46 A.M. (local time), American Airlines Flight 11 was flown into the north tower of the World Trade Center in New York City. Fully fueled, the aircraft exploded in an enormous fireball and set the upper floors of the building ablaze. This was just the beginning. At 9:03 A.M., United Airlines Flight 175 struck the south tower; at 9:37 A.M., the Pentagon in Washington DC was struck by American Airlines Flight 77; and finally, around 10:20 A.M., United Airlines Flight 93 crashed in a field in Pennsylvania.

By far the greatest death toll of that terrible day occurred in New York City. The intense heat of the fires caused the World Trade Center's south tower to ➤➤

KEY FACTS

September 11, 2001 – Four US airlines on domestic flights are hijacked. Two planes are flown into the World Trade Center, one into the Pentagon and another crashes in Pennsylvania.

The World Trade Center towers collapse, killing nearly 1,800 people.

The total death toll comes to nearly 3,000, and the events are the catalyst for a major US anti-terrorism campaign.

The south tower of the World Trade Center is hit by the second hijacked aircraft, while the north tower burns.

➤

collapse at 9:59 A.M., and the north tower also collapsed half an hour later. These two incidents cost the lives of 2,800 people, including around 400 police officers and firefighters and 157 people on the aircraft. In the Pentagon, 189 people were killed, and all 45 people aboard Flight 93 in Pennsylvania also died. The final death toll rose to 2,986, more than the total number of people who were killed at Pearl Harbor in 1941.

WAR AGAINST TERRORISM

The September 11 attacks have had a profound effect on the United States and the world in general. Under President George Bush, the United States began a massive, and politically controversial, global anti-terrorism operation. The United States and Allied nations subsequently went to war in Afghanistan and overthrew the ruling Taliban regime. Soon after the September 11 attacks there were terrorist attacks in Madrid and Bali, which are also said to be the work of al-Qaeda. ∎

Above: The fully loaded fuel tanks of the two airliners that crashed into the towers meant that there was enough heat in the fires to melt the structural steelwork.

Rescue workers stand in silent remembrance at Ground Zero. Up to 10,000 children in New York City lost one or both of their parents in the World Trade Center attacks.

INDIAN OCEAN TSUNAMI

ON DECEMBER 26, 2004, AN UNDERWATER EARTHQUAKE OCCURRED IN THE INDIAN OCEAN.

It was a huge seismic event, scientists estimating that it measured 9 on the Richter scale – the highest level of destructive force. The incredible release of energy even caused the earth to wobble on its axis. The earthquake literally ruptured the sea floor along the juncture of the Australian and Eurasian tectonic plates, causing the sea floor to shift upwards by several meters and in turn triggering a huge tsunami, which radiated out across the Indian Ocean.

OCEANWIDE DESTRUCTION

Traveling at speeds of up to 500mph (800km/h), but slowing and rising to a height of 32–50ft (10–15m) near land, the wave first hit the western Indonesia coastline, the closest destination to the epicenter of the earthquake. The resulting devastation was total, the wave sweeping away thousands of people and wiping entire coastal regions off the face of the map. This happened within 15 minutes of the earthquake, but the tsunami went on to cause death and destruction across the Indian Ocean over the next seven hours, wrecking coastlines as far distant as Somalia, some 4,500 miles (7,241km) away.

By the end of December 26, it was becoming clear that the tsunami had caused one of the greatest aquatic disasters in history. By February 2005, more than 150,000 people were confirmed dead, and the toll eventually rose to more than

KEY FACTS

December 26, 2004 – An earthquake measuring 9 on the Richter scale occurs in the Indian Ocean around 100 miles (160km) northwest of Sumatra.

The earthquake triggers a tsunami, which devastates communities as far away as 4,500 miles (7,241km) from the epicenter.

Current figures place the death toll at more than 225,000.

The tsunami races into shore as individuals in the surf fruitlessly run to escape the waters.

➤➤

225,000 victims. Indonesia was the worst hit, Sumatra being only 100 miles (160km) from the epicenter, and it lost 94,000-plus people; Sri Lanka lost an estimated 50,000; southeastern India, nearly 30,000; Thailand, 13,500 people; and other countries affected include Bangladesh, Myanmar, Malaysia, the Maldives and Somalia.

DISASTER RESPONSE

The tsunami disaster generated an enormous worldwide aid response. As we have seen in many examples throughout this book, the initial disaster may be just the beginning of the problem, and subsequent deaths from disease and malnutrition can far exceed those killed by the initial event itself (the tsunami left around 1.7 million people homeless). Today's international community has infinitely better medical and aid responses than the world had even 50 years ago, and we can only hope that new technology and medicines will prevent the scale of the disaster becoming any worse than it already is. ■

Above: Helicopter became the only viable method of reaching people in the most inundated areas. A typical air lift by a Sea King helicopter could deliver enough food to feed 727 people for a total of 30 days.

The earthquake under the Indian Ocean in December 2004 awakened the world to the full power of a tsunami. Coastlines bordering the ocean were turned into wildernesses, with many areas inaccessible to international rescue services.

Glossary

abject Utterly hopeless.

apocalyptic Related to end-of-the-world disaster or doom.

asphyxiate To kill or knock unconscious by depriving of oxygen.

besieged Under attack or distress.

burgeoning Growing or expanding rapidly.

charnel house Building or chamber for storing corpses and bones.

clemency Mercy or leniency in punishment.

epidemic Outbreak or product of sudden, rapid growth.

facilitate To make easier.

frenetic Frantic; in a frenzy.

harrowing Tormenting; worrisome.

havoc Wide destruction and confusion.

incendiary Involving the burning of property.

ingress Entrance or access.

inundation Flooding.

millennia Periods of a thousand years.

mortality rate Measure of the number of deaths over time.

pandemic Occurring over a wide area.

poignant Deeply affecting; touching.

pumice Volcanic glass.

pyroclastic Formed by fragmentation in a volcanic eruption.

quarantine To separate individuals from the population for a period to prevent the spread of disease.

zenith Highest point.

For More Information

National Geophysical Data Center

E/GC 325 Broadway

Boulder, CO 80305-3328

(303) 497-6826

E-mail: ngdc.info@noaa.gov

Web site: http://www.ngdc.noaa.gov/hazard/hazards.shtml

The National Geophysical Data Center plays a major role in collecting data following natural disasters. It also assists in the detection, location, and evaluation of the extent of certain hazards (including fires, floods, hurricanes and cyclones) using satellite data. The center's Web site also has disaster information specifically for students.

U.S. Department of Homeland Security

Federal Emergency Management Agency (FEMA)

500 C Street SW

Washington, DC 20472

(800) 621-FEMA; TTY (800) 462-7585

Web site: http://www.fema.gov/index.shtm

The primary mission of FEMA is to reduce the loss of life and property and protect the United States from all hazards, including natural disasters, acts of terrorism and other human-made disasters.

Web Sites

Due to the changing nature of Internet links, Rosen Publishing has developed an online list of Web sites related to the subject of this book. This site is updated regularly. Please use this link to access the list:

http://www.rosenlinks.com/wwid/hidi

For Further Reading

Bartoletti, Susan Campbell. *Black Potatoes: The Story of the Great Irish Famine*. New York, NY: Houghton Mifflin, 2005.

D'Silva, Themistocles. *The Black Box of Bhopal: A Closer Look at the World's Deadliest Industrial Disaster*. Oxford, England: Trafford, 2006.

Gallagher, Carole S. *The Irish Potato Famine* (Great Disasters: Reforms and Ramifications). New York, NY: Chelsea House, 2002.

Hanson, Neil. *The Great Fire of London: In That Apocalyptic Year, 1666*. Hoboken, NJ: Wiley, 2002.

Harris, Nancy, ed. *Great Disasters: Tsunamis*. Farmington Hills, MI: Greenhaven Press, 2003.

Kelly, John. *The Great Mortality: An Intimate History of the Black Death, the Most Devastating Plague of All Time*. New York, NY: HarperPerennial, 2005.

Macmillan Reference. *History's Most Devastating Disasters*. New York, NY: Macmillan, 2001.

Owens, L. L. *The Great Chicago Fire*. Edina, MN: Abdo, 2007.

Winchester, Simon. *A Crack in the Edge of the World: America and the Great California Earthquake of 1906*. New York, NY: HarperCollins, 2005.

Index

S

San Francisco earthquake, 6, 54–56
September 11, 2001, terrorist attacks of, 10, 68–70
septicemic plague, 26
slavery, 32–34
smallpox, 30
Spanish colonization, 29–30

Stabiae, Italy, 19, 20, 22
Sullivan, Daniel, 50

T

Thera, eruption of, 4–5, 14–16

U

Union Carbide, 64, 66

V

Vesuvius, eruption of, 19, 20–22

W

World War I, 53, 58
World War II, 10, 53

ABOUT THE AUTHOR

Dr. Chris McNab has published over 30 books on subject areas ranging from military history to human survival. His titles include *The Illustrated History of the Vietnam War, German Paratroopers of WWII, The Encyclopedia of Combat Techniques*, and *How to Survive Anything, Anywhere*. In addition, he has written dozens of articles for magazines, newspapers and encyclopedias, and he also works as a copy editor and proofreader. Chris lives in South Wales, UK.

WOODLAND HIGH SCHOOL
800 N. MOSELEY DRIVE
STOCKBRIDGE, GA. 30281
(770) 389-2784